W9-ALV-514

PERSIAN CATS

SANDRA L. TONEY

© T.F.H. Publications, Inc.

Distributed in the UNITED STATES to the Pet Trade by T.F.H. Publications, Inc., 1 TFH Plaza, Neptune City, NJ 07753; on the Internet at www.tfh.com; in CANADA by Rolf C. Hagen Inc., 3225 Sartelon St., Montreal, Quebec H4R 1E8; Pet Trade by H & L Pet Supplies Inc., 27 Kingston Crescent, Kitchener, Ontario N2B 2T6; in ENGLAND by T.F.H. Publications, PO Box 74, Havant PO9 5TT; in AUSTRALIA AND THE SOUTH PACIFIC by T.F.H. (Australia), Pty. Ltd., Box 149, Brookvale 2100 N.S.W., Australia; in NEW ZEALAND by Brooklands Aquarium Ltd., 5 McGiven Drive, New Plymouth, RD1 New Zealand; in SOUTH AFRICA by Rolf C. Hagen S.A. (PTY.) LTD., P.O. Box 201199, Durban North 4016, South Africa; in JAPAN by T.F.H. Publications. Published by T.F.H. Publications, Inc.
MANUFACTURED IN THE
UNITED STATES OF AMERICA
BY T.F.H. PUBLICATIONS, INC.

CONTENTS

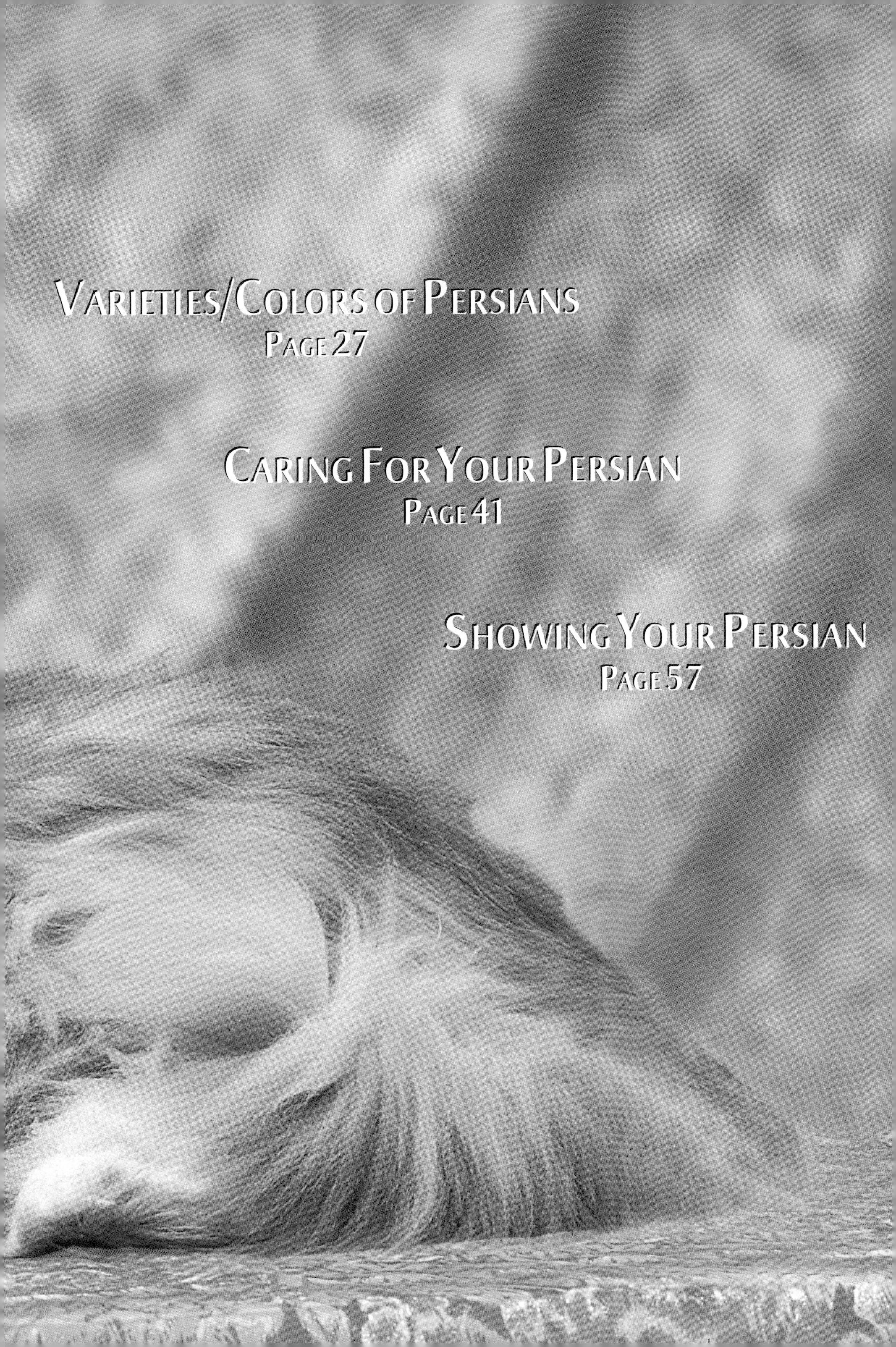

We do not know the exact origins of the Persian, how they came into existence or where they were developed.

HISTORY AND ORIGIN OF THE PERSIAN

If you're thinking about becoming (or perhaps already are) the proud owner of the most popular cat in America, the Persian, there are many aspects about this particular feline you may want to know. Where did this gorgeous creature come from? How is it different today than when first discovered? How should you care for, groom, and feed this special cat? And, do you want such a prized cat merely as a personal pet or to breed and/or show around on the competition circuit? Persians are a breed of cat all their own. First, you must discover their special qualities, unique habits, and other important facts before deciding if the priceless and beloved Persian is the right cat for you.

Throughout the ages, cat owners around the world have discovered the many benefits of befriending their furry feline companions. According to fossil discoveries, it is believed that cats first appeared some 35-40 million years ago. However, they probably weren't domesticated until approximately 5,000-8,000 short years ago (compared to 14,000 years of domestication for their canine counterparts). In Egypt, cats were actually worshipped as goddesses. The Goddess Bast, who was thought to control the heat of the sun, was depicted in a statue of a woman's body with a feline's head. Egyptians also believed the cat was the daughter of Isis and the Goddess of the Sun and the Moon, and that the glow from a cat's eyes held captive the light of the sun.

Cats were mummified alongside Egyptian pharaohs which undoubtedly proves that they were held in great esteem. Carved wooden figurines, jewelry and furniture—all in the form of the fair and revered feline—have been widely found among the relics of ancient Egyptian habitats. Cats are depicted in many ancient Egyptian hieroglyphics as well.

Besides possessing extreme beauty, most historians agree that humans found another advantage in the cat's presence in controlling rodent populations, and thus protecting precious grain and food supplies. Cats have proved to be an asset to virtually every community in which they've settled.

As the world soon discovered, all cats were not the

Look at that face! It's no wonder the Persian is the most popular cat breed in the world.

same. The mysterious feline came in all shapes and sizes, colors and temperaments. Until the early 1600's, the only cats appearing in Europe, as well as the rest of the world, had short hair. So, imagine the surprise and delight of those who encountered the first luxurious longhaired felines.

As difficult as it may be to speculate about exactly how Persians first found their way into civilization, we know that a man named Petro della Valle is accredited with introducing the first longhaired cats into Europe. Della Valle brought several pairs from the land of Persia (known today as Iran)

to Italy in approximately 1620, and hence they were named Persians, after the area in which they were discovered.

At about the same time, a Frenchman, Nicholas-Claude Fabri de Peiresc, brought longhaired cats from Angora (known today as Ankara), Turkey, back to his homeland. Like the Persians, these cats were dubbed Angoras because of their land of origin.

For many years following the discovery of longhaired felines, Europeans referred to all of these cats as Persians or Angoras (although there was a difference between the two breeds) and sometimes even

combined the names as one, the Persian-Angora. But there was indeed a difference between the Persian and the Angora felines—the Persian cats had fuller, woollier coats and were stockier, while the Angoras from Turkey sported a silkier coat of fur and a lighter frame.

As we know, most animals in the wild have always been able to adapt to all types of cultures and climates. So it is presumed that longhaired cats were the result of—or, perhaps, even a mutation of—cross-breeding between the furry European wild cat and the Steppe Cat, discovered by the German naturalist, Peter

For many years all longhaired felines were considered to be the same type of cat. Today there is indeed a difference—Persian cats have fuller, woollier coats and stockier bodies.

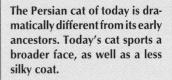

The Persian cat of today is dramatically different from its early ancestors. Today's cat sports a broader face, as well as a less silky coat.

The Persian is the world's most registered cat breed, and truly is the loveliest to behold.

Simon Pallas. Long, dense hair was quite necessary for these felines so that they could protect themselves from the cold Asian environments of Persia and Angora.

Longhaired cats soon became the rage in Europe, especially in England. British owners of longhairs, now called Persians or longhairs, created clubs based on color. Blue longhairs were the most popular color in the late 1800's, and even the British monarch, Queen Victoria, had a pair of the colorful blue felines.

In 1910, the Governing Council of the Cat Fancy (GCCF) was formed in England and the recommended standards of cat breeds were drafted. At that time, the Council decided that the longhaired felines known as longhairs, or Persians, would be known formally as

longhairs, thus entirely dropping the name of Persian. The Angora, however, declined in popularity because cat lovers preferred the Persians' fuller coat and stockier build to the Angora's slighter coat and leaner build. Today, this feline is known as the Turkish Angora, which enjoys nothing close to the following of the Persian breed.

Across the Atlantic, cat owners in the United States were obtaining these longhaired cats in abundance from England. By the early 1900's, the Persian, which was the name given to the American longhairs, had overtaken the once-popular Maine Coon Cat as the predominate longhaired feline to appear in the cat fancier's numerous shows.

The U.S. and Great Britain would ultimately differ in more than just the *name*

given to this unique and glorious cat. The Cat Fancier's Association (CFA), the leading cat registry in the U.S. and the world, was founded in 1906 and today sponsors over 400 shows around the globe. The CFA's standards for the Persian, and the GCCF's criteria— as well as how Persians were categorized into divisions—would ultimately cause much confusion to the novice and experienced fancier alike.

This prized cat was also bred in different structural directions, mainly in the areas of the head shape and nose break, and would soon become the object of much criticism and concern. Nevertheless, the Persian was—and still is—one of the world's most registered, highest rated, and truly *loveliest* of all felines to behold.

SELECTING YOUR PERSIAN KITTEN

The search for your Persian kitten is about to begin. There are many important things to contemplate, however, before undertaking this considerable task. You will need to know where to look and what you should be looking for prior to selecting your new furry friend.

First and foremost, you must understand that taking *any* kitten into your home is a commitment to care for, respect, and love this innocent creature for the duration of its life. Kitty will depend on you, its owner, for every need and want. Food, recreation, medical check-ups, grooming, security, and companionship are just some of the things your new kitten will require. Generally speaking, the above is true of any kitten or cat you would adopt, however, adopting a Persian feline will require more time and care than some other cats you could choose. Because the Persian coat is so long and full, your kitten needs your help in keeping it tangle-free and beautifully brushed. The Persian owner-to-be must understand that taking in a

This Persian litter, owned by Dot LaFlamme, is ready and waiting to steal its way into your heart.

Food, recreation, veterinary check-ups, grooming, security, and companionship are just some of the things your kitten will require.

special cat such as this will require daily grooming. So, you must count on spending at least 20 to 30 minutes each day taking care of your Persian's gorgeous fur coat. If you don't believe you have the time or energy to undertake this task of grooming, you may wish to rethink your decision to own this longhaired feline.

Once you have made the choice, that owning a Persian is something you desire, the next step is to decide where you can acquire such a pet. You have seen cats advertised in the newspapers. You have walked by the mall pet shop and witnessed their tiny faces stuck up against the glass.

Would the local shelter have any Persians ready to be adopted? You have even heard about people called "breeders" who specialize in producing specific breeds of felines. But where should *you* go to find your Persian kitten?

Most of the time, you will not see an advertisement in the newspaper by a person trying to sell or give away a purebred cat. In special cases, you might be able to pick up such a treasure, but you should be wary of such a cat because purebred owners are usually quite selective of where they place their kittens. Most of them would not advertise in such a way to the general public. Pet stores

have taken a lot of flack in the past few years and most experts will tell you not to buy any cat—pedigreed or not—from one of these so-called "kitten mills."

Pet store owners have been charged with getting their cats from undesirable suppliers who only care about how *many* kittens they can produce instead of the quality of kittens produced. Of course, it is possible to find a properly bred Persian at a pet store. As with everything else in this world, just because some pet stores get their felines from kitten mills does not mean they all do. You will want to do some serious checking, however, before purchasing a

These two little ones will depend on you for everything when they first arrive home. Be sure you are ready to accept the responsibility that owning a cat warrants.

kitten from a pet store. Do not be afraid to ask questions—lots of questions—and observe the surroundings of the pet store. Is it clean? How do all the animals look—sick or healthy?

Also, you should expect to be provided with the appropriate paperwork disclosing your Persian's genetic background. Find out if your kitten comes with a warranty, too, because the substantial cost of a purebred kitten (which could be anywhere from $200-$500) is a financial investment as well as an emotional one. If your kitten becomes sick or, worse yet, dies soon after you purchase it, what is the pet store's replacement policy under these circumstances?

Another place you might naturally look for a feline companion would be your local animal shelter. Because of the costs involved in raising pedigree cats, you probably won't find a Persian—or any other purebred for that matter—waiting patiently to be adopted at the city pound. Cats costing hundreds of dollars do not normally end up in a cage next to the many abandoned strays and homeless alley cats found each year.

What if you would like to own a Persian cat but do not really have the extra cash required to buy one from a pet store or breeder? That is where a fairly new type of establishment comes in—breed rescue organizations. There are several different types of these groups, and while some focus on specific breeds, such as Abyssinians, Ragdolls, or Persians, others are shelters for all general purebred felines.

At these breed rescue sites, you will probably not find an abundance of kittens looking for homes. Most of the cats at these organizations have been placed there as adults for various reasons: some have lost their homes due to an owner's death or perhaps a

How could anyone not love this little creature? You must understand that taking a kitten into your home is a commitment to care for, respect, and love him for the duration of his life.

A cup full of kitties—or in this case, a wine glass!

selecting your persian kitten

cross-country move where the family can't take their beloved pet. Left homeless through no fault of their own, these cats almost always make wonderful pets.

And, there are those who may not have the time or energy that a new kitten requires. Litter training, frequent feedings, teaching where to and where not to scratch, etc., takes some time. An adult Persian will be well-trained in most instances, and probably will not want to play with your big toe that is sticking out from under the covers at 3:00 a.m.

The downside of the breed rescue programs is that, in some cases, the papers providing your pedigree's background and parentage may not be available. If you are planning to show your Persian, you must have

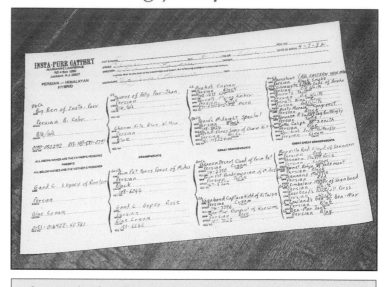

When you decide to buy a Persian regard your purchase as you would any other—you want a good quality product. A pedigree and registration certificate should be provided to you that include your kitten's parentage and pertinent cat association information.

New Persian owners must understand that selecting a cat with a full, buoyant coat will require daily grooming.

papers before you can register your cat.

If you just want a beautiful, classy companion at an affordable price (plus the simultaneous advantage in rescuing a homeless kitty), breed rescue organizations are definately something to consider.

When you think about buying your Persian kitten, regard your purchase as you would any other type of purchase. If you want a good quality product, you probably won't get it at your local discount department store (even though they may have the product in question, it most likely will be lower-priced and lower quality). However, if you want a good, dependable product with a reputation for reliability, you will want to go to a specialty store.

In fact, most people look for a specialist when they want the best quality or service.

Kittens can get into all sorts of hot water, or in this case, house plants. Be careful that your kitten doesn't get too adventurous—some house plants can be poisonous to cats if ingested.

Cuddle me! Every kitten needs somebody to love.

Finding your purebred kitten should be no different. If you want a good quality Persian, you will want to find a Persian specialist. This is where a reputable breeder comes in.

The word *reputable* is very important because anyone can breed an animal and claim to be a breeder. A reputable breeder, however, will be registered with one or more of the national or international feline registries, such as Cat Fanciers' Association (CFA), American Cat Fanciers' Association (ACFA), The International Cat Association (TICA) or one of the other registries.

Although your phone book may have a listing for local cat breeders, the best place to find a reputable breeder is at a cat show. Cat shows take place practically every weekend in cities and towns all over the world. They will usually be sponsored by one of the hundreds of cat clubs and will be a CFA, TICA, ACFA, etc. show, meaning the cats entered must meet the standards and criteria set up for the breeds in that particular registry (all registries have different rules and regulations). You can find out about upcoming cat shows in your area by looking in one of the cat magazines available.

Upon entering a cat show, you will see dozens of breeds of cats. Looking for a Persian,

Purchasing a Persian from a reputable breeder will ensure you a healthy cat with a good disposition. Visit the breeder and watch the kittens interact with their littermates, like the litter shown here.

Kittens, kittens everywhere! You will want to think long and hard before accepting the responsibility of owning a Persian. Once you've made up your mind, it can become an absolutely wonderful experience.

however, will probably be the easiest to spot and to find. Persians seem to stand out from the best of the breeds because of their long, luxurious coats and their almost "picture perfect" appearance. Even if you know virtually nothing about pedigree cats, you probably know what a Persian looks like because, due to their extreme beauty and class, they are widely used in television commercials and advertisements. Besides knowing what they look like, you'll probably see *more* Persians than any other cat because they are the most registered cat.

Persians are distinctive and regal. This calico Persian knows that he is the epitome of beauty and class.

Look at this litter owned by Dot LaFlamme. Is it any wonder that Persians are often used in television commercials?

Are you looking at me? This kitten's expression is a perfect example of the brilliant, sweet expression that Persians are known for.

These two-month-old blue smoke and cream Persians look as if they are just waiting for you to love them.

According to CFA's 1996 statistics (the world's largest cat registry), they account for more than two-thirds of all breeds registered. With these kinds of statistics, it is quite obvious that the Persian is indeed a very popular cat.

Obviously, breeders at a cat show will be showing cats that are registered (or they would not be there in the first place). Many of them place business cards on top of their cages for spectators and interested parties to take and use at a later date. A lot of breeders are willing to discuss the breed in general and, more specifically, their own cattery and the cats they raise. You can learn a lot from these breeders because they are in the business of producing beautiful, high-quality animals.

Some breeders will also bring kittens along from their cattery and have a "For Sale" sign outside of the cage. Don't make an impulsive decision and buy one right then and there. A breeder usually likes to get to know more about who will be taking home one of their precious newborns.

In fact, it is beneficial to both you and the breeder to learn more about each other before jumping into an agreement regarding a kitten. Of course, you'll want to know all there is to know about Persians before choosing yours, and the breeder will want to know about your intentions, as well, for the kitten. Will you be showing the cat? Using the cat to breed? Or simply taking it home and loving it as a dear companion?

Before buying your Persian kitten (or kittens), make sure you've done your homework. Visit the cattery where the kitten was born and raised. If a breeder is uncomfortable having you visit his cattery, you should exercise caution because the breeder may have something to hide.

A breeder who lets you visit and spend some time at his cattery would be your best bet. The cattery should look and smell clean. The animals

You'll want to know all there is to know about Persians before choosing yours—make sure you do your homework!

should be in clean, roomy cages or in a confined area (males and females should not be allowed to run together as this could cause questionable breeding results). All the cats should appear friendly and healthy. Signs of illness in any member of the group could spell trouble, as cats commonly pass diseases and illnesses to one another. You will want a breeder who actually spends time with the kittens and handles them daily. Early socialization with humans is crucial to a cat's overall personality. If you plan to show your Persian, it is especially important to choose a sociable cat who is used to being handled by a multitude of people.

Look at the mother (and father, if possible) and try to imagine what the kitten will look like as an adult. Also, the parents' behavior is a sign of how your kitten will behave as an adult. Cautious, unfriendly parents often raise (or contribute to) cautious, unfriendly kittens. Make sure you receive lineage papers and certificates as well as proof of inoculations and other important medical information. The entire atmosphere is very important in your ultimate decision of whether to buy a kitten from a particular cattery or not, so trust your instincts as well. Finding the perfect Persian kitten or cat for you means spending the next 10 or 20 years with this little fur-person. Make your decision an informed one.

Once you've found the right breeder, pet store, breed rescue organization, or other source for your Persian, there other considerations before choosing your kitten. Do you want a boy or a girl? Is there a specific color or pattern you'd like? More importantly, is the kitten you are interested in a *healthy* kitten?

Deciding on the gender characteristics of a cat is a rather difficult topic to ad-

Once you've found the right source for your Persian, there are other considerations to take into account before choosing a kitten. Do you want a boy or girl? Is there a certain color you prefer?

This kitten looks about ready for a nap. Always make sure the kitten you are interested in is healthy. He should appear clear-eyed and have a shiny coat.

Playfulness is a sure sign of a healthy kitten. These silver and silver cream kittens look as if they are ready for a good game!

dress. Some people believe there is a distinct personality difference between male and female felines. Others insist that, if neutered, there is absolutely no difference whatsoever. Of course, the difference between a whole female and intact male are very distinct, and, if you are going to breed your Persian, altering your cat will not be an option.

A female in heat is an unruly, desperate sight. Besides being extremely unhappy, she will try to escape the confines of her home or cage at every opportunity. She will cry very strenuously—and practically nonstop. A whole tomcat, however, is not much easier to live with. Male cats that have not been neutered (and, unfortunately, occasionally in some that have) exhibit a nasty, smelly habit known as spraying. It is an instinct used for marking territories. A male will also try to escape and probably be in a very bad mood for awhile. However, if

you want to breed your Persians, this is what you will have to live with and, eventually, become accustomed to, whether yours is a male or female feline.

The color and pattern of your Persian should be dictated by personal taste. Persians have numerous color and marking variations, so you will have plenty to choose from. Registries in the United States, such as CFA, will classify Persians in categories such as solids, bi-colors, etc, while in Great Britain, Persians are separated by color, with black Persians considered a breed, red Persions another breed, and so on. When selecting a pedigree, you will also need to decide whether you want to show the cat, breed the cat, or merely keep him as a pet in your home. These factors will be considered in the price of your Persian. Obviously, the most expensive and sought-after Persians are those that will be show cats. This "perfect" feline will adhere to all the

standards set by his particular registry.

Next in quality and price are those Persians who are not show quality, but can be used to breed. Finally, the least expensive, but equally charming and lovable, are the Persians who do not meet the registry standards as a show cat or breed cat. Only you can decide what purpose this Persian will assume under your ownership.

The most important factor in selecting your Persian is its health. Perhaps the easiest thing to spot is a sickly kitten or the so-called "runt" of the litter. A lot of people are drawn to the quiet, scared, wobbly-legged creature out of pity and sympathy. However, in selecting your Persian, you must not let pity enter in to this considerable decision. The breeder will make sure this little kitten gets stronger over time and will not abandon it. Your job is to find a healthy kitten who will live a long and happy life in your home.

In determining a kitten's

The color and pattern of the Persian you choose are merely your personal taste. Aren't these white Persians adorable?

The distinct personality of the Persian has always been highly regarded. Persians are gentle, quiet felines...a delight to own.

health, you must examine the cat very carefully. First of all, ask to see records of the kitten's vaccinations. He should have had all necessary shots before you take him home. Most breeders will not let their kittens leave the nest until they are at least 12 to 14 weeks of age, so it will have had plenty of time for inoculations and veterinary check-ups.

Your kitten's first sign of health will be his energy level. After observing the kitten in his usual surroundings, clap your hands or make a noise to catch his attention. Try to entice the kitten to chase a string or ball. An uninterested kitten may be an unhealthy kitten. If the kitten has litter-mates, notice how he relates to them. Does he jump right in and play with the others or does he hover in the corner? You will want a lively, energetic kitten who is attentive and curious.

A physical check will be next on your list: a healthy kitten should not have the sniffles or runny nose or eyes. The gums should be a healthy pink and the teeth a clean white. The kitten should be able to breathe normally and shouldn't have a cough. Also, beware of the haw (a.k.a. the third eyelid) if it is shown partially covering the eyes, this is a telltale sign of illness in cats.

Check the rear of the kitten for signs of diarrhea. A kitten that has diarrhea will most likely have dirty, wet and matted fur around its bottom. The body of the kitten should be uniform without its ribs sticking out or a pot belly, which is a sign of worms. You should even check the kitten's

In determining a kitten's health, have your veterinarian examine the cat very carefully. All kittens should receive the necessary vaccinations before you bring them into your home.

ears for mites, which look like little specks of pepper or coffee grounds inside the ear. Also, the ears should not have wax or dirt in them. The kitten's skin should be smooth and devoid of scabs and splotches, and the fur should be fuzzy and healthy looking, not dry.

Overall, if you have thoroughly researched the Persian, and explored your options in terms of how and

where to purchase your kitten, you will have found a loyal, loving and stunning companion with whom to share your life. Surely, you will never forget the time, love, and energy involved in selecting your perfect Persian kitten. Not to worry, though, because your Persian, as with *any* respectable, proud feline, will spend the rest of his days reminding you.

You will never forget the time, love, and energy involved in selecting your perfect Persian kitten, and your Persian will spend the rest of his days reminding you!

Varieties/Colors of Persians

If you would love to own a Persian, you aren't alone. In fact, the Cat Fanciers' Association's (CFA) 1996 statistics list the number of Persians registered in that organization at approximately 42,500. But that number is even more astounding once you realize that there were only 68,948 cats registered *overall*. More than two-thirds of CFA-registered felines are classified in the Persian breed division.

Because most feline pedigree registry organizations classify their cats differently, you will probably want to start off by studying the world's largest organization, (the Cat Fanciers' Association) and their rules for classifying Persians. Separated into seven different color divisions, the registered Persian must fit into one of the following categories to be considered for CFA competition in the Persian class.

SOLID DIVISION

To register your Persian in the Solid Color Division of CFA, your solid feline must have a coat that finds each hair the same color from its root to its tip, without any markings or shadings. Standard Persian colors are black, white, blue, red, cream, and, the still rather uncommon shades of lilac and chocolate. Solid black Persians must have bright eyes of copper color and their coat must be shiny with an almost polished-looking appearance. Of course, their nose pad and foot pads must be solid black as well.

Persians registered as solid whites must possess a glowing white coat without appearing yellowed or stained. The white Persian's nose and foot pads should be a healthy pink. The eye color of the white Persian, however, can vary. Gleaming copper eyes are acceptable as well as a deep, vivid blue color. (Keep in mind that white cats with blue eyes are often deaf.) The other acceptable eye color is

This black Persian is a member of the Solid Color division. Blacks must have bright eyes of copper color, and their coat must be shiny with an almost polished-looking appearance.

Persians registered as solid whites must possess a glowing white coat and a nose and foot pads of a healthy pink.

that of one copper and one blue eye. This unusual feline is called the Odd-Eyed Persian and is always a sight to behold.

Blue Persians were once the most prized of all Persians. Even Great Britain's Queen Victoria owned a pair of Persian blues. To the unaccustomed eye, the blue feline may be referred to as gray but, in actuality, the coat of the blue Persian exhibits an almost "diluted" blackish-gray appearance, thus known in the cat fancier world as blue. As for the eye color, copper is the standard.

The red Persian is a somewhat controversial cat because many Reds are of the peke-faced variety (which is frowned upon in Europe because of health concerns), which means their noses are extremely sunken in, much like a Pekinese dog. The red Persian's foot pads and nose leather are the same flame-colored red as its beautiful coat which, by the way, is not

The blue feline may be referred to as gray, in actuality the coat of the blue Persian exhibits an almost "diluted" blackish gray appearance, thus known as blue. Copper is the standard eye color.

The lighter the coloring of the cream Persian, the better. Nose and foot pads should be pink and the eyes a brilliant copper color.

The red Persian is an orangish/brick color with nose and foot pads of the same color. Copper eyes complete the package.

BI-COLOR DIVISION

A bi-color Persian will consist of a white coat with one or two other colors "patched" onto it. Only two patched colors at most are allowed on the white background of the bi-color Persian. The word, "bi," which means two, may lead fanciers to believe that only white and one other color patched on the cat would be admissible. However, this is not the case because the multi-colored calico is included in the bi-color division.

Other color combinations include tabby-and-whites, solid-and-whites, smoke-and-whites, and vans. No more than two-thirds of the coat should be colored and no more than half of the coat should be white. The solid

a bright "apple" red, but almost an orangish/brick red. Copper eyes complete the red Persian package.

As far as the cream Persian is concerned, the lighter the cream shade, the better. As with the white Persian, the nose and foot pads should be pink. The eyes need to be a brilliant copper.

Lilac is a rarely seen variety of Persian. The standard lilac should be a warm tone of lavender with a touch of pink in his coat. Copper eyes, along with lavender or pinkish foot pads and nose leather round out this unusual feline. As with the lilac Persian, the seldom seen chocolate Persian is also a product of crossing a Persian and a Himalayan. The coat should appear as a warm brown or "chocolate" color, with a slightly lighter brown nose and foot pads and copper eyes.

A bi-color Persian will consist of a white coat with one or two other colors "patched" onto it. The solid color of the cat should form an inverted "V" on the face with the rest remaining white.

The calico Persian should actually be a member of the tri-color group, but it is shown with the bi-color. There are two types of calicos—regular and diluted. This diluted calico exhibits lighter patches of blue and cream.

Another variety of the bi-color Persian is the Van pattern. A Persian Van is bi-colored with most of the cat being white, and the colored area confined to the tail, head and sometimes the legs.

eyes will be obvious as well.

The calico Persian should actually be tri-colored rather than bi-colored, but is shown with the bi-colored Persian class. There are two types of calicos — regular and diluted. The regular calico is a white feline with intense patches of black and red, while the diluted calico exhibits lighter patches of blue and cream. Once again, copper eyes are favored. It should be noted that, except in rare cases, the calico is always female.

The final variety of the bi-colored Persian is called the van pattern. A Persian van is bi-colored with most of the cat being white, and the colored area confined to the tail, head and sometimes the legs. One or two small patches of the same color are allowed on the main part of the body. With copper eyes, the Persian van is either black and white, red and white, blue and white, or cream and white.

PARTI-COLOR DIVISION

A parti-color Persian is a feline with several colors, none of which is white. Four varieties of parti-color Persians make up this division: tortoiseshell, chocolate-tortoiseshell, blue-cream, and lilac-cream. Parti-colors will almost always be female (but in the rare event a that male parti-color is born, it will normally be sterile). Copper must be the eye color in all these Persians.

A tortoiseshell Persian exhibits a black body with well-defined patches of red and cream scattered throughout the coat. A flare of red and cream from nose to forehead is preferable in the face. Tortoiseshells (also known as

color of the cat should form an inverted "V" on the face with the rest remaining white. Also, you shouldn't find any white hairs hidden in the solid parts of the colored coat.

One would normally think of a bi-colored Persian as this standard solid-and-white variety. This particular Persian commonly displays a white underside, chest, muzzle, as well as parts of the feet and legs. The white can be complemented with black, blue, red, cream, chocolate, or lilac. Brilliant copper eyes round out this Persian variety.

The tabby-and-white Persian is accepted in the standard tabby division colors. Like the solid-and-white Persians, the inverted "V" is desired as well on the white chest, muzzle, underside, feet and legs, except for the silver tabby, who can have green or hazel eyes, and the tabby-and-white Persian, who should have copper eyes.

Smoke-and-white Persians should follow the same rules as those applied to the tabby-and whites except the tabby parts will exhibit one of the smoke color varieties. Copper

varieties/colors of persians

torties) are one of the more expensive types of Persian because they are so difficult to produce.

The chocolate-tortoiseshell, which differs from the regular tortoiseshell, has a chocolate brown body with well-defined patches of red. A diluted tortoiseshell Persian is known as a blue-cream Persian. The body is blue (diluted black) with clearly outlined patches of diluted or pale cream. Finally, the lilac-cream Persian presents a beautifully colored pinkish- lavender feline with clearly outlined cream patches.

TABBY DIVISION

Tabby cats have been around for many years. In fact, people sometimes refer to cats in general as "tabbies." Tabby is actually a pattern of cat rather than a color, and all cats have tabby genes in their background (although other traits may hide the tabby markings). The Tabby is characterized by its brilliantly distinct markings and patterns. Generally, the Persian breed is a laid back type of feline, with the tabby being the most outgoing and extroverted variety. All Tabbies have copper eyes except for those with silver coats, who may have green or hazel eyes.

The classic tabby is recognized by the bull's eye markings on the side of the body. The coat has broad, dark markings winding across a lighter shaded body. The legs and tail should have dark, circular rings around them. Rope-like necklaces should encircle the upper chest and neck. A complex line forming a pattern resembling the letter "M" should appear on

Tabby is actually a pattern of cat rather than a color. All cats have tabby genes in their backgrounds.

the forehead. Accepted colors are silver, red (including the peke-faced), brown, blue, cream, cameo, cream cameo, and blue silver.

A mackerel tabby should have thin—as opposed to broad—markings in the classic tabby pattern, including barred rings around the legs and tail. Thin, rope-like necklaces should also be apparent on the neck and upper chest. The letter "M" should also appear on the mackerel tabby's forehead, as in the case of the classic tabby. The accepted colors are the same as the classic tabby.

The patched tabby Persian, known as the torbie, is actually a tortoiseshell tabby with the usual red and cream patches but will have a tabby-colored background instead of black. The patched tabby can exhibit the mackerel or classic pattern, and appears in the same recognized colors, except for the shades of red, cream, and cameo.

A parti-color Persian is a feline with several colors, none of which is white. This tortoiseshell Persian exhibits a black body with well-defined patches of red and cream scattered throughout the coat.

SILVER AND GOLDEN DIVISION

The silver and golden division and the shaded and smoke division are perhaps the most complicated of all divisions to comprehend. These cats have coats that are "tipped," which means that some or all of the hairs are tipped with a different color at the tip than at the base of the hair.

Perhaps no other cat will ever be as striking once you've witnessed the chinchilla Persian. The silver and golden division includes the chincilla Persian as well as shaded silvers and goldens. The chincilla is a glistening white feline with black or gold tipping lightly sprinkled throughout the entire coat, except for the pure white chest and stomach. There are both golden and silver varieties of chincilla Persians. It is surmised that the name chinchilla comes from the rodent of the same name in South America, who has a similarly colored coat.

One confusing aspect of the silver and golden division comes from the shaded silver Persian, who is basically a silver feline with just a bit more tipping and shading than the chincilla. In fact, many cats who are classified as shaded silvers often mature into actual chinchilla Persians.

The shaded variety of Persian exhibits a mantle of black on its backside, with evenly shaded sides. Of course, there should be darker tipping on the legs and face than is found on the chinchilla. Golden Persians have a basic color that is a deep, warm cream with the tips of the hairs being black.

Both silvers and goldens should have green or hazel eyes with a black rim encircling them as if a makeup artist had applied eye liner to them. The nose should be either a dark red or rose colored and the paw pads should be black.

The silver and golden division and the shaded and smoke division are the most difficult distinctions for a beginner to comprehend. This silver Persian has a black rim circling his eyes, as if he's wearing eye liner!

The shaded variety of Persian exhibits a mantle of black on his backside, with evenly shaded sides, like this shaded silver Persian.

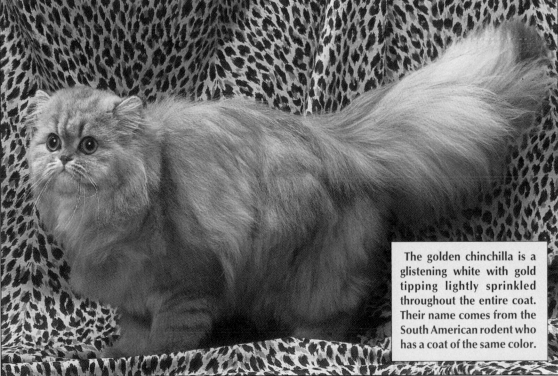

The golden chinchilla is a glistening white with gold tipping lightly sprinkled throughout the entire coat. Their name comes from the South American rodent who has a coat of the same color.

Golden Persians, like this one, have a basic color that is a deep, warm cream with the tips of the hairs being black.

SHADED AND SMOKE DIVISION

The shaded and smoke division contains all Persians with tipped coats, except for those who are found in the silver and golden division. Smoke Persians, in black, blue, cream, cameo (red), smoke tortoiseshell, and blue-cream fall in this category as well.

A smoke Persian is a beautiful sight to behold. When you first see a smoke Persian lounging or sleeping, it will appear that the feline is a solid color Persian. Once the smoke Persian begins to move, however, you will be able to see the undercoat, which is a pure snow white.

The smoke Persian is a bit of a surprise. When not in motion, the smoke Persian appears to be solid, but once he begins to move you will discover an undercoat of snow white! This blue cream point female is owned by Dot LaFlamme.

The shell cameo is a Persian with the white undercoat but the hairs are lightly tipped in red. The shaded Persian finds hairs moderately tipped with black, red, golden brown, or a combination of red, black and cream. Copper eyes are the norm in Persians in the shaded and smoke division.

Overall, the shaded and smoke and silver and golden categories are rather difficult to differentiate. Of course, the whole business of understanding the world of purebred felines requires a great deal of study and observation if you plan to master this particularly complex part of the cat fancy.

HIMALAYAN DIVISION

The Himalayan, one of the most popular felines in the cat fancy world, is the result of breeding the stunning, longhaired Persian with the vocal, pointed-patterned Siamese.

A longhaired Persian with the points of a Siamese was the outcome (although a Siamese is no longer needed to breed the Himalayan). Defining exactly where this feline belongs, however, has become a controversial and difficult task.

The Cat Fanciers' Association considers the Himalayan a division of the Persian breed, much as the solid and parti-colors are divisions of

Persians. Most other associations in the United States and abroad, however, view the Himalayan as its own breed of cat. Regardless of the category in which the Himmy (as it is affectionately nicknamed) belongs, this cat is a stunning creature and graciously accepted by cat lovers around the globe.

According to CFA standards, all Himmys must have piercing blue eyes and the traditional "Siamese" colored points on the face, legs, feet and tail. The remaining coat color can be anything from white to fawn.

The array of approved point colors for the Himalayan include: lilac, blue, red, cream

The Himalayan is one of the most popular cats in the feline world. Originally a result of breeding the Persian to the Siamese, the Himalayan has raised much controversy in the cat associations.

tortoiseshell, chocolate, seal, blue-cream, chocolate-tortoiseshell, lilac-cream, seal lynx, blue lynx, red lynx, cream lynx, tortoiseshell lynx, blue-cream lynx, chocolate lynx, lilac lynx, chocolate-tortoiseshell lynx, and lilac-cream lynx. As diverse as the cat itself, recognizing and remembering the many color variations present a real challenge to breeders and observers alike.

UNITED STATES AND EUROPEAN DIFFERENCES

Registering and showing your Persian in the United States is quite a different experience than in Europe (mainly Great Britain) where the practice of showing cats is thought to have originated. By far, the most radical difference between U.S. Persians and those in Great Britain is the acceptance and encouragement of the "peke-faced" Persian by U.S. cat fanciers. The red peke-faced Persian is described as looking much like a Pekinese dog, with a pushed-in, flat face and nose. Other varieties of Persians in the U.S. also exhibit the pushed-in facial features, but none quite radically as the red peke-faced Persian. It is interesting, to also note that one U.S. cat registry association, the Cat Fanciers' Federation (CFF), even classifies the peke-faced Persian as a separate breed altogether.

In Great Britain, however, the Governing Council of the Cat Fancy (GCCF), Britain's largest cat registry association, discourages the breeding of the peke-faced Persian (or any Persian for that matter) with extreme flat facial features, because of health problems associated with this type of Persian.

Veterinarians have even expressed concern over the peke-faced Persian's potential health problems, and, in fact, the GCCF actually considers it a facial deformity. These felines frequently experience sniffling and breathing problems as well as eating problems if their lower and upper teeth do not bite together correctly. Also, the tear ducts may be blocked, causing persistently runny eyes. In Great Britain, the Persian is encouraged to have a regularly proportioned face, known as the Doll-Face.

Obviously, a good and careful breeder can produce peke-faced and flat faced Persians if bred correctly. Many of these Persians never experience any health problems and the misconception that *all* Persians are basically unhealthy is simply a myth.

There are several differences between the cat fancy of the United States and Europe. The encouragement of the peke-faced Persian in the U.S. is frowned upon elsewhere.

The breed name differs between U.S. and British registries in the actual naming of this cherished longhaired cat. The British sometimes simply refer to them as Longhairs, while Americans prefer the more distinguished title of Persian, after their assumed country of origin.

Another difference between U.S. and British registries is the actual naming of this cherished longhaired cat. The GCCF simply calls this cat a longhair, while the U.S. prefers the more refined title of Persian, after its assumed country of origin.

Perhaps the most striking distinction between a CFA cat show and a GCCF cat show is the class in which you register your Persian. If you take a black Persian to a CFA cat show, it will be registered as a Persian breed, in the solid division. However, if you take that same black Persian to a GCCF show, you will register this cat as a black longhair breed. This is on account of the way the GCCF has divided its longhairs, or Persians, into breeds.

Each *color* of Longhair/Persian is classified as a different breed. As in the CFA, where a black Persian will compete against white, red, blue and other solid color Persians, the GCCF black longhair will compete only against *other* black longhairs. Likewise, black smoke longhairs will only compete against other black smoke longhairs.

Many people think this is a good idea because they believe there are actual *structural* difference between the colors. Of course, the odds of winning in the black longhair competition is greater for your cat if you are not competing against all the other black longhairs as well as the *rest* of the solid color divisions—- blue, white, red, etc. longhairs. The Himalayan, too, is a separate breed in the GCCF known as a colorpoint longhair.

Finally, whether you call your fluffy feline friend a Persian or longhair; register it as a Persian in the solid division or as a certain color breed of longhair, it's still your most loyal friend, and an integral part of your devoted family. So, it does not really matter what you call your longhaired, luxurious feline, as long as the two of you are *together* at the end of another eventful or boring, difficult or leisurely, yet always glorious day.

It doesn't really matter what name you give your cat, as long as the two of you are happy sharing your lives together.

CARING FOR YOUR PERSIAN CAT

Once you have selected your Persian kitten, you will hopefully have many years ahead to love and care for it. Of course, caring for your Persian properly includes having the right knowledge and the proper tools as well as a loving home and safe environment. You must remember that your Persian demands extra care and attention because of its special needs and requirements, especially in the area of grooming. First, however, you must have the necessary supplies and equipment when introducing your new Persian kitten into your home.

NECESSARY CAT SUPPLIES

Before your Persian kitten arrives, much like before you bring home a new baby, you will have to prepare your home for the newcomer. You will of course need some type of food and water bowls, a litter box, grooming supplies, a place to sleep, a sturdy scratching post, and perhaps the most important thing of all, plenty of kitty toys to occupy their days and nights. A cat carrier is also extremely important for the times when you must transport your cat.

FEEDING

If your Persian is still a kitten, you must take that into account when purchasing the first food and water containers. Be sure that they are the correct height and size because little kittens need bowls low-to-the-ground yet wide enough so they won't be tipped over easily. Also, try to place the bowls in a low-traffic arca so your cat can eat in peace and quiet rather than in the middle of the kids' bowling alley.

The material your bowls are made out of count, too. As many cats are quite finicky about certain types of food, they also care about the container they eat from. Plastic bowls sometimes emit an odor and can cause feline acne if the rim gets rough or cracked. Ceramic can contain lead and can break. Stainless steel seems to be the preferred choice because it is easy to clean and dishwasher-safe. Sterility of the bowls, of course, is the most important factor of all. The cleanliness of your cat's bowl should equal the cleanliness of your own eating utensils.

Treats can be provided on an occasional basis to help create a little variety in the diet. Some treats act as a cleaning agent to help reduce tartar on the cat's teeth. Photo courtesy of Heinz.

caring for your persian cat

Cats need fresh water at all times. Make sure you change the water daily and keep the water dish accessible to every cat in your household. If the cats go outside (which they should *not* do because cats, especially Persians, are not

When placing your feline's food and water containers, make sure they will be easily accessible to your cat, in a quiet area so he will not be disturbed when eating.

equipped to deal with the elements, bugs, cars, other animals, and the variety of hazards that the great outdoors present to today's

There are two options when considering the feeding of your cat. Some people prefer to leave food accessible at all times, while others feed two meals per day. Whichever your decision, it is important that your cat receive a healthy, balanced diet.

felines), don't assume they can drink out of a mud puddle or a nearby lake. Every cat needs a clean bowl with fresh water at all times!

There are two options when considering the feeding of your cat. Some people prefer to leave food out 24 hours a day so their cat can nibble anytime he feels hungry.

Plus, this method avoids the 3:00 a.m. "Wake-up-I'm-hungry" calls from a famished feline. Other people, however, fear their cats will become overweight if allowed free access to food all the time so they feed their cats on a schedule. Beware, however, of being 10 minutes past schedule because, whether you

Did anyone hear the dinner bell? These guys sure did! Remember, if your cat depends on you for his meals, he will want to be served promptly!

An important thing to keep in mind when caring for your Persian is that he depends on you for everything. This little kitten needs your attention, love, and kindness to ensure he has a good, long, healthy life.

believe it or not, cats *can* tell time. Whichever manner you prefer should probably receive your veterinarian's approval. Your veterinarian can also assist you in deciding what type of food your cat requires. Different stages in a cat's life demand different nutritional needs. Kittens need different types of nutrients than senior cats. Also, certain vitamins and minerals found in quality cat food can help keep your Persian's glorious coat in top-notch condition.

Finally, try to give your Persian access to some greens. Most pet stores carry flats of grass already planted or else you can buy grass seeds of your own to plant in an indoor pot. Of course, any houseplants should be off-limits and out-of-reach because many types are poisonous, and, in some cases even deadly, to kitty!

You will also want to supplement your Persian's diet with some type of lubricating gel or cream to help with hairballs. Obviously, a cat with such a thick coat will have problems with hairballs. Some people give their cats a pat of butter everyday while others purchase a tube of this mint-flavored gel from their pet store or veterinarian.

LITTER TRAINING

Almost any cat instinctively knows to use a litter box. When you introduce a new cat into your house, the *first* place you should point out is the litter box. And don't try moving it around for decorating purposes. Pick a spot and leave it or else kitty might decide to use its favorite "bathroom" location whether the box is there or not.

It is important to realize that cats are creatures of habit. They don't appreciate change in any of their nine lives. So, buying a certain brand of litter because it is on sale can invite the nasty habit of having your cat decide not to use the litter box anymore. If you find a good brand of litter that your cat likes (i.e. *uses*), your best bet is to stick with that particular litter to avoid any problems later.

Location is significant as well. Try to place the box in a secluded, out-of-the-way area. Also, kittens may need a smaller box at first so they can easily climb in and out of it easily. As the cat matures, a bigger box will be necessary. The litter boxes with hoods are probably the best choice because some cats can be standing inside the litter box yet actually eliminate outside of it (say, on your new carpet). A litter box hood will prevent that scenario as well as give kitty privacy.

The number of litter boxes is crucial as well. The general

Anyone can recognize a well-fed cat. He will appear healthy with an alert expression and a smooth, gleaming coat.

rule is to have one litter box per cat. Cats don't like sharing their box with each other, although in a multi-cat household, the dominant cat will usually "mark" all the boxes in the home to show who is in charge. Regardless, the more boxes, the better.

Because cats are fastidiously clean animals, you must keep their litter boxes tidy as well. You can purchase an inexpensive scooper that you can use to dispose of solid waste daily, but be sure to change the litter as often as necessary. If the box is dirty, your cat might decide to find more suitable facilities (like your freshly laundered bedspread).

Almost any cat instinctively knows how to use a litter box. Cats are fastidiously clean, therefore their litter boxes must be kept so as well.

It's as important for our animal friends to have healthy teeth and gums as it is for us. Fortunately, maintaining oral care is getting easier and easier for pet owners. Now there's a taste-free, easy-to-use gel that will keep pets' teeth clean, reduce tartar build up, and eliminate breath odor. Photo courtesy of Breath Friend/ American Media Group.

caring for your persian cat

GROOMING

The first thing you will notice about your Persian cat is that he sheds. And not just a little— he sheds a lot. So if you hate the thought of having cat hair everywhere in your home, do not get a Persian. If you only wear the color black when getting dressed, don't get a *white* Persian. Cat hair of "contrasting" colors are like magnets drawn to your favorite clothing.

The second thing you will notice about your Persian is that, if not groomed properly and on a daily basis, its beautiful, long fur coat will become tangled and matted. Then, the coat is not so lovely anymore. The best way to avoid matted fur and an

Because of their long coats, Persians will need special care when it comes to grooming. Be prepared to spend adequate time with your feline in the pursuit of a well cared for coat.

"Okay mom I'm ready for my bath, or maybe a nap!" This Persian kitten doesn't seem at all bothered by the thought of a bath.

You have to admit that this fella doesn't look too pleased. Thank goodness giving your Persian a bath is only necessary occasionally!

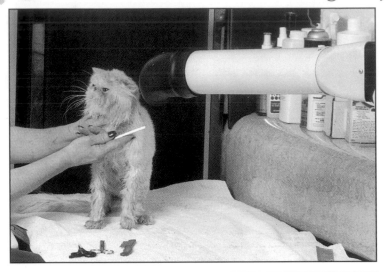

Make sure that after your Persian's bath he is dried thoroughly to avoid any chance of catching a cold or chill.

its own coat as many other cats do through self-grooming. The Persian has been bred in such a way that human assistance is required to keep the Persian coat tangle-free. If you want your Persian's coat to be in top form all the time, you should comb the cat every day. Starting this daily regimen when the cat is young will make it easier for both of you in the years that follow.

It will be helpful to have two types of combs—one fine-toothed and one with wide teeth. Start out by combing the entire cat with the wide-toothed comb and then go over it once more with the fine-toothed comb. If your Persian experiences any tangling or matting, try to gently break the knot into smaller pieces with your fingers. Only cut the knot out as a last resort, and be careful

overabundance of shedding is to stop these problems before they start. Regular grooming will become your salvation.

Before the grooming process begins, you will want to trim your cat's toenails to prevent being scratched. If started at a young age, your Persian will get used to grooming and having its nails trimmed—even if it doesn't necessarily *like* it! You should trim a cat's claws approximately once a month. Carefully place the cat on his back in your lap and, while holding the cat securely, gently press down on the paw so that the nail comes out. Then, with a pair of clippers from your pet store or veterinarian, clip off the tip of each nail just outside the pinkish part where the nerves are stored. If you cut into the "quick" part of the nail, considerable pain and bleeding will take place. If you feel uncomfortable performing this procedure, your veterinarian or local groomer should be able to do this for a small fee.

After the nails have been clipped, you are now ready to groom your Persian. These cats have such an abundance of fur that it is nearly impossible for the cat to take care of

Make sure that your grooming routine includes regular attention to the eyes, nose and ears.

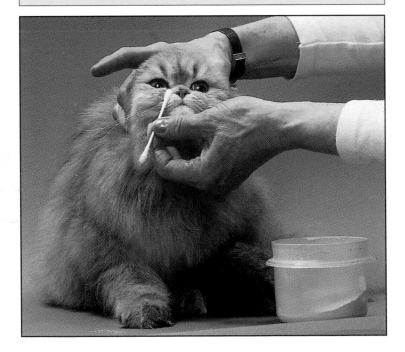

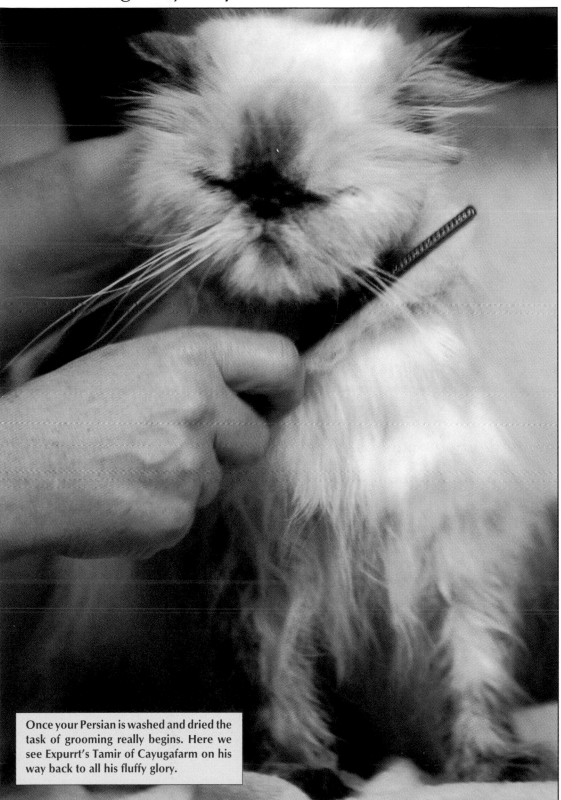

Once your Persian is washed and dried the task of grooming really begins. Here we see Expurrt's Tamir of Cayugafarm on his way back to all his fluffy glory.

not to let the scissors touch the cat's skin, which pierces more easily than you might expect.

Giving your Persian a bath is only necessary occasionally. Of course, cats that are shown in competition will be bathed more often. Too much bathing can dry out a cat's skin. If and when you decide to tackle the chore of bathing your Persian, make sure the water is lukewarm and use an appropriate shampoo approved for cats (which can be acquired from your pet store or veterinarian). Be careful not to get shampoo in the cat's eyes, nose, ears, or mouth. In fact, the head should be kept dry during the bath and, afterwards, wipe the head area off with a warm, damp cloth. You can either let your Persian's coat air dry in a warm room or use a hair dryer (but only if your cat is comfortable with this). Finally, your cat will look like new!

SCRATCHING POSTS/THE DECLAWING ISSUE:

All cats have the urge or need to scratch. For this reason, if you want to save your furniture from being shredded, you will buy or make a scratching post for your Persian. The best type of post is one securely fastened vertically to a base and covered with either carpet or a rope-like substance called sisal. The post should be tall enough so that your cat can stretch upwards the entire length of its elongated body. Besides activating the glands in their paws that act as territorial markers, scratching also removes the dead part of the toenails, so don't be surprised if you find little pieces of kitty's toenails scattered around the scratching post. The most convincing way to entice your cat to use the post is to rub it with catnip.

As for declawing, almost all experts now agree that you should *not* declaw your cat. Besides making the creature utterly defenseless, it can also cause psychological problems. Imagine having a gun with no bullets. Not very effective protection, is it? This is the way a cat without claws feels. Clipping them often and teaching them to use the scratching post is a much more humane method of deterring cats from unfavorable scratching habits.

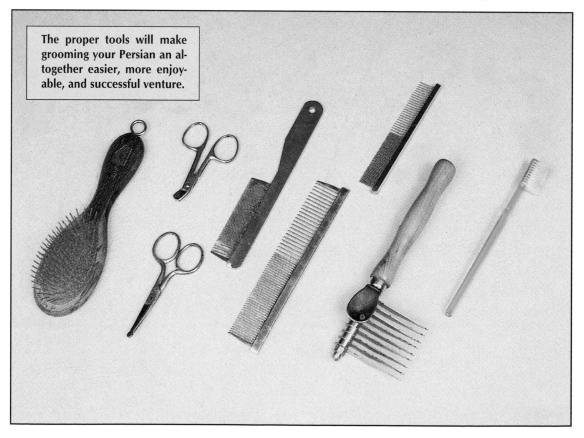

The proper tools will make grooming your Persian an altogether easier, more enjoyable, and successful venture.

All cats have the need to scratch! No, they don't just enjoy destroying your furniture. To keep this from happening, every cat should be provided with a scratching post.

TOYS

A healthy cat is a playful cat. However, the Persian cat is considered one of the most relaxed and docile felines in the cat fancy. Perhaps because they are so ornamental, they do not like to get their fur ruffled or soiled. Whatever the reason, there will be times when your Persian will get that ornery look in its eyes and proceed to attack everything in sight.

If you don't want your bare toes to become your cat's prey, you will want to make sure that there are plenty of cat toys around to peak that curiosity cats are famous for. Although there are aisles and aisles of cat toys in your local pet store, department store and supermarket, some of the best kitty delights can be found right underneath your nose.

Any object that rolls, such as an empty spool of thread or the cardboard remains of a used-up toilet paper roll or paper towel roll are perfect examples of inexpensive amusement for the feline in your life. Those plastic rings that come off the lids of gallon milk jugs will delight any cat for hours. Wadded up balls of foil or old socks are other suitable diversions.

Also, cats love to hide, and Persians are no different. Empty paper sacks make the most annoying and loud noises, yet your cat will find much pleasure running in and out of them just to produce those crinkling sound effects. Also, plastic sacks make fun hiding places (just make sure you cut any handles off plastic and paper sacks to prevent your cat from getting his head stuck and possibly choking).

A healthy cat is a playful cat. Make sure to provide your cat with plenty of toys to amuse him. Otherwise, you know what they say about cats and curiosity....

Luckily, there are aisles and aisles of wonderful toys in your local pet store that will be sure to amuse your cat for hours.

String is another attention-grabber. A long piece of string tied onto a stick or broom handle can amuse kitty for quite some time as you swing it back and forth while watching television. Of course, any toys, such as string, that could be a hazard to your cat (like getting tangled up in it) should be put away when you are not around and only brought out for your cat when someone is there to supervise.

GENERAL HEALTH CARE:

Good health care will make a world of difference to the health and happiness of your Persian. The very first step in health care is acquiring a qualified, trusted, and knowledgeable veterinarian. This veterinarian is the one you'll depend on to take care of your Persian in sickness and in health (much like a good marriage). Preventative medicine, including regular check-

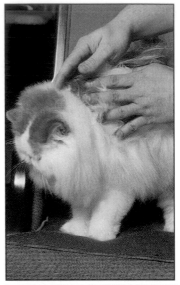

Make sure that any trip to the veterinarian includes a complete and thorough physical examination of your Persian.

Some of the best kitty delights can be found right under your nose and need not be store bought items. You will be amazed at the fun your cat will have with plastic bottle caps or anything that rolls.

ups and vaccinations, will ensure your Persian a long and prosperous life.

The veterinarian you choose will be up to you, of course. You can always choose a well-known, popular clinic or, as an alternative, you can choose a housecall veterinarian, an emerging field of veterinary care which is gaining in popularity with pet owners. A housecall veterinarian will come to *your* home and take care of your pets. This reduces the stress of traveling to a clinic as well as avoiding the many illnesses that your cat can encounter in an office setting. The final decision is yours, but as a loving pet owner, you should consider all aspects of veterinary care available to your cat.

Whenever you travel with your cat, whether it is to the veterinarian's office or to a cat show, you will want to place him in a sturdy cat carrier during the trip. Some people think that their cat is so tamed and well-behaved that a carrier is not needed. However, all it takes is one second for your cat to jump from your arms while being carried into the veterinarian's office and you may never see your beloved again. Cats startle quite easily, so don't take that chance. The best protection is prevention.

Keeping your Persian healthy also means regulating the possible hazards in his life. If you let your Persian go outside, you have lost all control over this area. Cats in general have no business

outside because there are too many dangers.

Persians especially, are not equipped for the lifestyle of an outdoor cat. A Persian's coat is just too long and delicate to hold up to the winds and weather Mother Nature presents. And, what keen flea wouldn't love to take harbor in the luxurious surroundings of a Persian cat? A screened-in porch or shelter is the perfect alternative to letting your cat outside. It is just too dangerous a world out there.

Unfortunately, Persians are sometimes prone to certain illnesses, especially the pug-faced variety. The most com-

mon ailments to look for are respiratory problems (breathing difficulties) and a frequent discharge from their eyes due to blocked tear ducts. Also, because of the long coat, constant self-grooming can lead to hairballs and even intestinal blockage. This can be minimized, of course, if you groom your Persian daily to help get rid of any excess hair that could be consumed by the cat.

As long as your Persian has regular veterinarian visits, vaccinations, and grooming, you should expect your cherished friend and companion to be around for quite some time.

Preventive medicine, including regular checkups and vaccinations, will ensure your Persian a long and enjoyable life.

BREEDING VS. ALTERING

In today's world, the overpopulation of pets has become somewhat of a problem. If every cat owner were a responsible cat owner, we wouldn't have this problem. Many people, however, do not have their cats altered and allow them to run free and mate several times a year which, in turn, leads to many unwanted kittens The statistics of innocent cats being put to sleep simply because they do not have a home are startling. We can all stop this problem by having our female *and* male kittens altered as soon as they come of age. Not only does this solve the overpopulation dilemma, but altered cats also make much better pets because they are not being ruled by their hormones.

If circumstances present themselves and you decide you would like to become a Persian breeder, you will have to follow the basic procedures for breeding that are set up by the registry or clubs in which you will register your Persian kittens. Breeding is not a business that should be taken lightly.

Normally, only a few experienced breeders ever make a monetary profit at breeding. You have to have the "perfect" queen matched up with the "perfect" stud to even have a chance at producing show-quality kittens. Plus, the time and money involved in this procedure is hardly worth the effort for most people. If you do decide to breed your queen, she must be at least one year old and should only have two litters a year at maximum. You should not breed unless you have good, responsible homes for all the kittens that will be born. You should also talk to other breeders before launching into this complex venture. Although it is rewarding to produce show-quality kittens, it isn't an easy task and should not be jumped into without thinking long and hard about whether you are really ready to bring more kittens into this world.

You should not breed your Persian unless you can guarantee good, responsible homes for all of the kittens produced. Millions of animals arrive in shelters each year through no fault of their own. Altering your animal is a responsible decision.

SHOWING YOUR PERSIAN

There is no doubt that a well-groomed, healthy Persian is one of the most beautiful creatures in the world. For some reason, you almost think they somehow are aware of that fact, too. If you decide you want to enter the fascinating world of the cat fancy, where you take your Persian on the road to compete in cat shows, there are many things you must know prior to entering that first show.

CHOOSING A REGISTRY

Before you register your cat with an association, you should know that there are several possibilities and, if you wish, you can register your Persian with more than one of those registries.

Of course, the biggest registry in the world, as well as the most widely known, is the Cat Fanciers' Association (CFA), which was started in 1906 and, to date, has registered over one million felines. The benefits of registering your Persian in this association are many, the greatest being its world-renowned recognition. It also established the Winn Feline Foundation, a foundation which funds research and studies in developing exceptional feline health.

The American Cat Association (ACA), the oldest cat registry in the United States, was established in Chicago in 1899. The ACA's goals are to support pedigreed cats as well as their owners by overseeing cat shows and maintaining a studbook registry. Known as the association of "firsts," the American Cat Fanciers Association (ACFA), founded in 1955, was the first association to hold double, triple and quadruple championship and grand championship rings. ACFA was also the first registry to accept altered cats for championship competition (against other altered cats, of

There is no doubt that a well-groomed Persian is one of the most beautiful sights in the world. If you decide that you would like to enter the wonderful world of the cat fancy, there is much you need to know.

course). They were also the first association to require prospective judges to complete written exams before being licensed.

In 1961, the first Canadian cat registry, the Canadian Cat Association (CCA), was born. Until that time, Canadian cat fancier's had to register their purebreds with American or European associations. Today, CCA boasts over 110,000 registered felines and accepts household and altered cats as well as pedigrees.

The Cat Fanciers' Federation (CFF) was organized in 1919 and today its shows often benefit animal welfare organizations and humane societies. CFF was the first association to award breeds not currently recognized for competition in the Any Other Variety (AOV) division. CFF oversees cat shows, keeps ancestry records and trains judges to abide by and uphold CFF ethics.

Four years after CFA was formed in the United States, England formed its first cat registry in 1910 called the Governing Council of the Cat Fancy (GCCF). It was this Council that decided to refer to Persians as longhairs. Of course, the GCCF doesn't agree with some of the U.S. standards set for Persians, such as the snubbed nose and face (which the British call "over-typed") but, instead, favors a traditional, doll-faced Persian.

The largest European cat sanctioning body is the Feline International Federation (FIFE), which includes many countries in Europe, Asia, South America, Australia and others. FIFE is more strict in its categories of faults, and strongly discourages any genetic defects in the Persians. They also recognize many colors and patterns not recognized in other registries.

The International Cat Association, Inc. (TICA) is the world's biggest genetic registry of pedigree and household cats. TICA, formed in 1979, adopted the unprecedented process of a judging format that doesn't mention status, title or identification of show entries. Cats are judged entirely on their merits at the time of judging.

PERSIAN STANDARDS

Regardless of the association in which you choose to register your Persian, the standards will most likely be very similar, except for the controversial pug-face versus doll-face issue. In this instance, we will use the standards set by the Cat Fanciers' Association as an example.

In the show ring, your Persian will be judged on seven different points with the total number of points equaling one hundred, which is a perfect score for the perfect Persian. The point breakdown is as follows: 30 points for the head, including size and shape of eyes, ear shape and set; 20 points for the type, including shape, size, bone, and length of tail; 10 points for the coat; 5 points for balance; 5 points for refinement; 20 points for color (in Tabbies, points are divided into 10 for markings and 10 for color and for bi-color Persians, the points are divided into 10 for "with white" pattern and 10 for color); and 10 points for eye color.

The CFA standard for a Persian head is one that is round and immense with a fullness to the skull. The neck should be short and compact with the head set firmly upon it. The Persian's face should be round with big, round eyes set far apart but level. A rounded chin and full cheeks and jaws should be present. Rounding out the "roundness" of the Persian head should be small ears with round, not pointed, tips, and they should be set far apart and low on the head.

Of course, the main object of controversy between the associations (mainly between European and American ones) is the nose. In the CFA, the nose should be snubbed and broad and have a break between the eyes. Other associations (such as the GCCF in Great Britain) prefer a more traditional Persian, *without* the snubbed nose and break between the eyes.

The most descriptive word used by people when explaining a Persian's body type is probably the word, "cobby." You can expect to see a full, stocky body with short, strong legs and large, round paws, including five toes present on the front paws and four toes on the back. The Persian's tail should be rather short, but proportionate to the rest of the body and, also, the tail should be lacking a curve and at an angle lower than the back. Also, the cat should be well-balanced and the eyes, ears, tail, legs, etc, should all seem proportionate to the overall body. A well-groomed Persian coat should resemble that of a lion's mane—long, full, and with a remarkably thick texture. The fur should also have a glimmering shine to it with a long ruff continuing down between the front legs. Long tufts of fur coming from the ears and between the toes are also desirable in the Persian. Owners should brush their feline so it appears as full and majestic as possible.

The word "refinement" in regard to the Persian almost seems redundant. Persians seem to be the epitome of refinement and grace. Of course, judging a cat on this standard is a difficult job because each person's idea of refinement may be different. This standard basically is the overall "feeling" the judge has about the entire Persian as a whole and complete cat.

Finally, the judge will determine the score of the coat coloring and eye coloring and how profound and flawless each of those qualities are on your Persian.

Unfortunately, there are some areas of imperfection in certain Persians that will be cause for disqualifying marks. A locket or button (areas of white on a cat that shouldn't have any white) found on the cat is one reason. Other disqualifying causes include incorrect number of toes, incorrect eye color, a weakness in the rear area and hind legs, bone deformities in the spine or skull, pointed Persians with white toes, a crooked jaw, crossed or crooked eyes, and nose leather placed incorrectly on the face.

Overall, your Persian should give the impression of complete and total "roundness," and his face and eyes should illuminate a sweet expression. This shouldn't be a difficult task because the Persian's basic personality is one of sweetness and serenity.

COMPETING WITH YOUR PERSIAN:

Once you register your cat with a cat registry association, you are then allowed to enter this animal in any cat shows sponsored by the particular registry. Remember, you can register your Persian in as many associations as you like, but it would be wise to read up on each association's rules and even visit some of their shows before making your final decision.

Once registered in a feline registry, you will be ready to start showing your Persian in competition. During the course of cat showing, however, your cat will be entered into different divisions depending on age and number

When it is your Persian's turn to be judged, he will be taken out of his show ring cage, be held up in the air, gently tossed around a bit, and given a toy to see how playful he is.

of points accumulated at previous shows.

There are also different types of show rings. In a specialty show ring, only felines with a similar coat type or length compete for awards (such as all Abyssinians) while in an allbreed show ring, *all* cats, regardless of breed, compete for the numerous awards.

Obviously, when you get a Persian kitten, you will probably want to start showing him in the "Kitten Competition." Your kitten will compete against other Persian kittens of the same sex and color for first, second, and third place ribbons. There aren't any breed or division awards in the kitten competition, but there are best and second best of color class awards given. This will familiarize your Persian with shows at an early age. To qualify, your cat must be between the ages of four and eight months old to compete and can be either altered or unaltered.

In the world of the adult cat fancy, competing felines must be whole, or unaltered. The exception to this rule is the class called the "Premiership Competition." In this class, neutered males and spayed females can compete and be judged under the same rules as those of whole cats in the other divisions. The only difference, of course, is that these have been altered. Because there are not as many cats competing in this division, less points are needed to become a Grand Premier.

Through the years, many people found that they did not have the time or money to own purebred cats so, unfor-tunately, they could not participate in the fascinating world of cat shows. Now, however, anyone who has a cat can become a part of this exciting pastime. The creation of the "Household Pet Competition" has opened the doors to all cat fanciers. In this division, any type of cat can compete as long as it is altered (if it's over eight months of age) and not declawed. These cats, of either gender, any age or length and color of coat, are judged for their beauty, "uniqueness" and disposition. All participants receive an award of merit and the best household pets are presented in the finals.

The most popular division at any cat show is called the "Championship Competition." In this category, whole, registered, adult felines from the 35 breeds currently recognized by the CFA compete for two titles at the show—-Champion and Grand Champion. Your adult Persian will start his "Championship" career in the Open Class where it will compete against other Persian of the same gender and color or type.

After your Persian makes it through the Open Class, he is eligible to start competing in the Champion Class for points towards that elusive tittle of Grand Champion. Once your Persian has earned 200 points, after winning numerous competitions such as Best of Breed or Division or Best of Color, it finally acquires the title of Grand Champion.

Of course, *all* cats entered in the show must be healthy, be fully vaccinated, whole (not altered), except for those competing in the Premiership class, and the household pet class. All cats must have their claws (i.e., have not been declawed), but the claws should have recently been trimmed to prevent scratching of the judges and handlers.

It is truly exciting to have your Persian win at any show. He will be awarded a first, second, or third place ribbon, as shown here.

Your cat will be placed on a disinfected table and thoroughly examined by the judge to see how he measures up to the breed standard, a written description of the ideal Persian cat.

AT THE SHOW

Your first cat show can be quite intimidating. It is best to attend some shows as a spectator—without your cat—before entering your first one. Once you've registered your cat, paid your fees, and been assigned a number, you will be expected to arrive at the show during the check-in time. You will then go to your designated spot and put up the curtains you brought (which CFA requires) for the top and three sides of the benching cage (except the front, obviously). This is to prevent cats from constantly looking at their neighbors and getting unduly upset.

Depending upon the show, your entry fee may include certain things as free litter, food and other minor items but it is best to always be prepared and have everything your cat will need with you (just in case the litter runs out or your cat refuses to use the foreign litter). You should also bring the cat's own food and water from home. You would also be wise to bring along your own spray bottle of disinfectant so you can disinfect your hands before touching your cat to prevent any danger of spreading disease or illness. If you're a breeder, you may want to bring business cards or a photo album of some of your Persians at home.

After your cat is settled in its benching cage, the judging should begin shortly thereafter. Make sure you know your cat's call number so you can move your Persian to the show ring quickly after it is called. There will usually be multiple rings with judging going on simultaneously. Once in the show ring cage, all the cats competing will be judged one by one by a qualified judge. When it is your Persian's turn to be judged, he will be taken out of his show ring cage and placed on a disinfected table while the judge examines him. Your cat

Without a doubt, showing your Persian can be a fun and rewarding experience for both you and your feline friend.

This cat looks as if she doesn't need a judge to tell her what she already knows—she is a champion!

will be held up in the air, gently tossed around a bit, and offered a toy to find out how playful he is. So, hopefully, your Persian will answer the call to stardom graciously and not be intimidated by the hundreds of pairs of eyes watching him.

When the judge is finished looking at all the competitors, the ribbons will be awarded to the judge's choices. The judge is supposed to be impartial and not know who the owner of the cat is or who bred the cat. The ideal cat show will acquire judges who pick the best cats solely on the feline's own merits.

Without a doubt, showing your Persian can be a rewarding and fun experience for both you and your cat. It will enhance your appreciation for cats in general and, if you are lucky, give you a few ribbons or trophies to proudly display in your home. Even if kitty never wins one prize on the circuit, however, there is one thing of which you can be certain: this devoted Persian is a Grand Champion in the only show that really matters—the one in your heart.

Showing your Persian may give you a few ribbons and trophies to display in your home, but remember, your devoted Persian is a champion in the only show that really matters—the one in your heart.